SHAMANISM

SHAMANISM

—

Meet your powerful
healing allies

SUZANNE EDWARDS

SIRIUS

For Ross Heaven, rest in power.

Image on page 155 courtesy: Alamy.
All other images courtesy: Shutterstock.

SIRIUS

This edition published in 2020 by Sirius Publishing, a division of
Arcturus Publishing Limited,
26/27 Bickels Yard, 151–153 Bermondsey Street,
London SE1 3HA

ISBN: 978-1-83940-676-8
AD008215UK

Printed in China

Contents

Introduction

Shamanism links us strongly to the Earth, the heavens, everything around us, and our own deeper layers. Through shamanic practice, we establish a connection that is beyond ourselves. The modern world fosters a sort of disconnection that is causing humanity a lot of suffering. In modern shamanic practice, we learn to journey, communicate with our guides, and receive guidance for ourselves. This empowers us. There are also many other aspects to shamanism to explore and play with. There's enough to keep us occupied for a lifetime. It's non-dogmatic and encourages creativity. It's about taking back the power for ourselves, for the Earth, and for our communities. We open ourselves up to altered states of consciousness, which are liberating and healing. It encourages us to tap into abilities and resources from the world of spirit that go beyond the rational mind. The rational mind is necessary for day-to-day living, but we also need to develop the other side – intuition, imagination, creativity and a sense of the sacred – if we want to become fully rounded human beings. Shamanism gives us the opportunity to do this.

Shamanism is rich, complex and ever-changing, much like the world we live in. Indigenous practices vary all over the world. Some have mutated and assimilated with religion and colonizing cultures. Some have been re-invented. Some have been lost entirely.

There is a reason for the strong interest and focus on shamanic practice that goes beyond it being just another fad to feed spiritual consumerism. The human soul is feeling a yearning, a calling, towards this. Shamanic practice is within all of us. It's within our genetic memories; it's within our ancestral DNA. Our ancestors are calling upon us to remember the true nature of reality.

CHAPTER 1

What is shamanism?

S hamanism is the oldest spiritual practice on the planet. It has existed in every part of the world. The noun shaman comes from the word *saman* from the Evanki tribe, a Tungus-speaking people of Siberia. It means 'to know' or 'to heat oneself'.

This is an umbrella term that has been coined in the West to describe these worldwide practices. However, more local and specific traditions, for example in parts of Africa or the Amazon, would not use the terms shaman or shamanism. Although these words will be used throughout this book, there are differences in practices between different traditions. These words are being used for convenience and for general understanding.

The shaman is a doctor, medicine man/woman, social worker and priest/priestess of the community, and is highly revered and respected as they carry a position of great responsibility. They have the ability to enter trance states and travel within the spirit realms to find information or assistance from spirit helpers to solve problems within the community, to provide healing for the sick, and to assist with escorting lost souls of the dead to the afterlife.

Historically, alliances with spirits would be made to bring forth rain to help crops grow and, in hunting cultures, information on where and when to find herds of animals. Shamans also presided over rites of passage such as birth, death, marriage, and coming-of-age ceremonies.

The shamanic view of reality is about connection and communion with the spirits that reside in everything. All humans, animals, plants, rocks, rivers – even things that appear to be inanimate objects – have a spirit/consciousness. This interaction enables the shaman to do their work and bring harmony where needed for this intricate interconnection between all forms of life on the physical and non-physical planes. This viewpoint can go to very profound levels in some traditions. For example, for the Taoists (whose roots are steeped deeply in shamanism), each organ in the body has unique spirits. The liver alone is said to have three spirits that are called The Hun. So, imagine how many spirits there would be to make up a single person?

Shamans were chosen often by inheritance, spontaneous 'calling' or 'election'. This could be through contact with an ancestor or spirit in a dream delivering the message. Other indications could be having extra

toes, fingers or teeth. Sometimes they would put themselves forward of free will, or by appointment of their clan, but such shamans were considered less powerful. For some, this was not a role or life that they desired as it could involve difficult and dangerous initiation processes that could last for years and with no guarantee of passing successfully.

Shamanic practice involves accessing ecstatic trance states with the use of drums, rattles, various instruments, singing, dancing, fasting, sleep deprivation, sweat lodges and, in some cultures, ingestion of hallucinogenic plants in ceremonial situations. A more expanded state of mind is reached – almost a state of 'no mind' – giving freer access to communication with the spirit world and a vision state. Healing can also occur when the spirits give information on why blockages and disharmony have occurred. The shaman can use this ecstatic state for 'magical flight' to retrieve missing soul parts and power that clients have lost due to stress, trauma or even displeased spirits.

Giving offerings to the Earth and for ancestors is also key as the concept of give-and-take is important in shamanic work. It is honouring the Earth and our ancestors in a symbiotic relationship. It can involve building altars and creating sacred spaces.

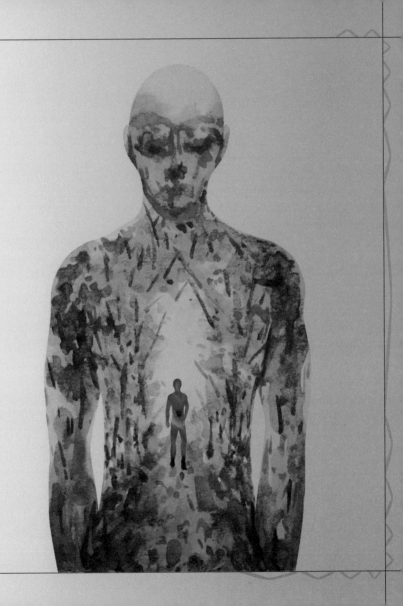

Initiation

Initiation is a crucial feature in the becoming of a shaman. There are various ways this can occur:

A sickness initiation

The shaman-to-be becomes extremely sick physically (or sometimes mentally) and sometimes in ways that cannot be cured by the usual means. During this sickness they can receive tutelage by spirits on how to cure themselves and for their shamanic training.

A near death experience

This can also be part of the sickness initiation, but not necessarily. There is a powerful link between shamans and the land of the dead. Such an initiation helps the shaman form that connection.

Being struck by lightning

This is a common initiation event all over the world. In the Altomesayoq Q'ero tradition, the shaman needs to be struck three times for validation of their shamanic status.

Resistance to cold

This is naturally often featured in initiation rituals for those in colder

climes. For example, the Inuit would sit in an igloo, in isolation, fasting for many days, waiting for ecstatic flight as a sign of successful initiation.

An ability to produce heat

An internal fire within the body can also indicate a shamanic calling. It is something that is also taught in certain Chi Gong traditions using breathing techniques and direction and collection of Chi.

Ritualistic tree climbing

This form of initiation was also common since this is a representation of the shamanic flight. One example being the Araucanian Machi of South America where a tree that had had its bark stripped was climbed by the shamaness. It was nine foot tall and is called a rewe or rehue and it was kept in front of her house. The ritual goes on for several days. A drum circle and dancing are formed around the tree. Her family sacrifices lambs. Cuts with a quartz knife are made to the lip and fingers of both the initiating shamaness and the apprentice. The wounds would take a week to heal.

A vision quest

On the North American plains they would take a vision quest out into the wilderness to pray and fast for a few days. The idea was that a guardian spirit would be received, often in the form of an animal. The initiate would take on the strengths and qualities of this animal and would teach them their medicine songs and what to put in their medicine bundles.

Visionary dismemberment by spirits

This terrifying vision is classic in many cultures. The shaman-to-be has visions of their limbs being torn off. Eyes, organs and sometimes blood is taken out in these visions and then replaced (sometimes with crystals). This was the marking of the removal of blockages and fears that would impede the person in their becoming of a shaman.

These experiences were often not one-offs, but would happen whenever the next stage of development was being reached, since there were often different levels of shamanic ability and standing. There was a strong

element of fear in these experiences and some of them are extreme. This was to bring the initiate face-to-face with fear to be overcome. They are brought to a new level of strength and power with fewer limitations. The attainment of spiritual power and gifts was also the purpose of these events. Shamanic sight was asked for. The replacement of eyes was to facilitate that request and was undertaken so that the new eyes would see differently with the gift of shamanic sight.

Sometimes formal initiation wasn't deemed necessary as some were born into the role and showed the necessary signs of shamanic seeing and dreaming, and did not need to pass a test. Spontaneous ecstatic trances were also confirmation of being chosen by the spirits.

One of the criticisms that contemporary shamanism has faced is that there is an absence of initiation and that the crossing over the abyss of fears is important. There are some teachers who do include initiatory aspects. Walking over hot coals is a popular one and another is being buried in a hole in the ground overnight. In these modern times some of us can really benefit from these initiatory processes as we have lost connection with these important events that help to build our characters.

Shamanism: past and present

S hamanism can be traced back to Paleolithic times and there are cave paintings around 30,000 years old depicting shamanic practices.

Traces of it are found all over the world, but in particular Northern Asia, the Ural Altaic, the Americas, the Arctic, Australia, New Zealand, Africa, Northern Europe, South-East Asia and the Far East. Shamanic practices are found today among Aboriginal Australians, Maoris in New Zealand, the Dagara and San People of Africa, Native American tribes, and the Sami people of Northern Europe, among many others. It began with hunter-gatherer communities and was continued in some societies even after the coming of agriculture.

Shamanism was prevalent all over the world but, as the world changed with the increasing spread of religious practices associated with monotheistic religions and colonization, it has rapidly decreased over time. Shamanic beliefs and practices were in fact aggressively targeted through warfare that suppressed indigenous cultures. Shamans were also persecuted by missionaries and their practices were outlawed.

In the seventeenth and eighteenth centuries the Buryats in Siberia strongly resisted Soviet colonization and their tribes were always led by a shaman. There were arrests and even executions of shamans in the 1930s because of this leadership role. However, these shamans persisted because they felt a strong need to protect their native way of life.

In China shamanism was prevalent until the Song dynasty (960–1279) where it rapidly declined while Taoism and Confucianism took over. Taoists began to gain more influence in the courts. Taoists also viewed the shamans as competition as they were employed to perform many of the same rites and exorcisms. As mentioned earlier, Taoist practices are deeply steeped in shamanism. The Confucians viewed the shamans as low

Paleolithic cave paintings have been found that show drumming and other shamanic practices to help with the hunt and daily life.

class, since the shamans were mostly illiterate. They sought to suppress them because they saw them as opposing their way of life and believed that their practices were barbaric. Some were executed and some were permitted to practice, but only under restricted conditions. Poor people still sought their assistance as they could not afford the doctors and medical experts that were replacing them.

In Latin America indigenous people who followed a shamanic way of life, with the advent of colonialism, were subjected to forced mass baptism, torture, enslavement, and murder. The Mexicans foresaw the stark future of what was upon them and they acted to preserve their knowledge and take it underground so that it could be brought out again when the time was right.

In the face of destruction and suppression, shamanic knowledge and wisdom has changed and adapted with the times and through the challenges it has been faced with.

In Latin America there is now Curanderismo, which is a blend of Spanish Catholicism and Aztec and Mayan practices. In the Caribbean, you have Santeria, Haitian Vodou and Obeah, all of which use Christian imagery and symbolism combined with African traditions. These are just some examples. As with time and human nature, we learn to adapt and mutate. Shedding our skin is the ever-changing nature of life.

There are some preserved unbroken traditions in existence. The Huichols of Mexico, who are the guardians of the Blue Deer Peyote plant medicine, and the Q'eros of Peru are both examples of this preservation. Thanks to their geographical locations, both being situated in very high mountainous regions, made them less accessible to the Spanish invaders. Likewise, there are tribes that have not succumbed to modernization, such as the Dogon people of West Africa, Yanomami of the Amazon, and the Korowai tribe of Papua New Guinea.

On the other side of all of this is Western society, where our roots and connection with these traditions have been almost completely eliminated. There has been a growing interest in reconnecting with that knowledge and wisdom. In 1932 John Neihardt published *Black Elk Speaks*. Black Elk was a medicine man of the Oglala Lakota people. In it he discusses his religious beliefs, visions, and his life story. This gave the West some positive coverage of Native American religion. In 1951 Professor Mircea Eliade's book, *Shamanism: Archaic Techniques of Ecstasy*, first published in French, also brought a lot of attention to the subject. It is one of the first truly comprehensive books to discuss the worldwide phenomena of shamanism and is still widely regarded, and referred to, today.

Then Carlos Castaneda, in 1968, released *The Teachings of Don Juan*, the first of twelve books from the late writer. He was an anthropologist who went to study the ethnobotany of the Yaqui people in Northern Mexico. He became the apprentice of Don Juan Matus, a medicine man, and wrote books recounting his apprenticeship and subsequent succession after Don Juan's death. How much of his writing is fact and how much is fiction is debatable, but the impact and influence of his books is undeniable. With more than 28 million readers, he opened many people up to the potential of shamanism. The hippy movement of the 1960s also sparked a huge interest in hallucinogenic plants and, during this time, Castaneda's accounts of Peyote and Jimson Weed would have been a source of fascination for many.

Michael Harner was another person who brought a lot of attention to the benefits of shamanism in the West. Also an anthropologist, he lived with and studied the people of the Upper Amazon, Mexico, Peru, the Canadian Arctic, Samiland, and western North America. In the '50s and '60s he took part in ayahuasca ceremonies in the Amazon. Those ceremonies were said to set the course for his path. In 1980 he released *The Way of the Shaman* in which he founded Core Shamanism. Harner, essentially speaking, created his own system of shamanism based on his studies of the features that linked different traditions and therefore could be likened to a core practice. Repetitive drumming to induce a trance state and facilitate a shamanic journey is the key factor in his system. He set up the Foundation for Shamanic Studies, which also supports indigenous cultures to preserve their traditions and gives them resources to be able to pass that knowledge on to the next generation.

Now we see elders and shamans from around the world travelling to teach westerners their wisdom. Trips and retreats are arranged to experience ceremonies, and sometimes training too, making spiritual tourism a thriving industry.

The story of the Four Nations is told by the Hopi people as well as other cultures. That we were one people and Great Spirit split us into four nations and gave us different skin colours. Black for the South, Red for the West, Yellow for the East and White for the North. There are prophesies that we will unite and teach each other our knowledge, bringing peace and healing to the Earth.

Due largely to the damage done by colonization, there is a lot of controversy surrounding contemporary shamanism. There are issues around cultural appropriation and some healers have protested at the sharing of practices, customs and ceremonies without permission and out of context. I would advise doing some research on your journey. Walk forward lightly, sensitively and with consideration, and the spirits will help you.

CHAPTER 2

The World Tree

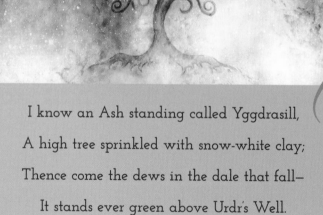

I know an Ash standing called Yggdrasill,

A high tree sprinkled with snow-white clay;

Thence come the dews in the dale that fall—

It stands ever green above Urdr's Well.

*From The Prose Edda by Snorri Sturluson,
translated by Arthur Gilchrist Brodeur*

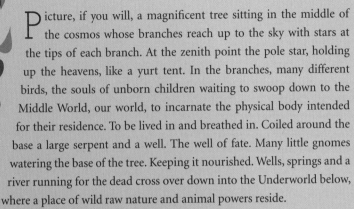

Picture, if you will, a magnificent tree sitting in the middle of the cosmos whose branches reach up to the sky with stars at the tips of each branch. At the zenith point the pole star, holding up the heavens, like a yurt tent. In the branches, many different birds, the souls of unborn children waiting to swoop down to the Middle World, our world, to incarnate the physical body intended for their residence. To be lived in and breathed in. Coiled around the base a large serpent and a well. The well of fate. Many little gnomes watering the base of the tree. Keeping it nourished. Wells, springs and a river running for the dead cross over down into the Underworld below, where a place of wild raw nature and animal powers reside.

The World Tree is the axis mundi, centre point of the shamanic landscape. The connecting point of the three worlds – Lower, Middle and Upper Worlds – and the four cardinal directions. Different traditions vary, the Toltecs of Mexico have thirteen heavens and nine underworlds and the Norse have nine worlds all over the tree. But for the purposes of this book we will use the three worlds. This is based on the neo-shamanic understanding of Siberian shamanism.

The tree is be climbed or descended by shamans. Shamans use the ecstatic state to make these journeys, for healing, receiving information, and retrieving power. We will be covering and exploring different ways to do this throughout the book. Features such as ladders, rainbows and vines are ways of travelling up and down the tree. Think of the biblical Jacob's Ladder in the book of Genesis where Jacob has a dream of angels descending and ascending a ladder that connects Earth and Heaven.

Odin's sacrifice

P erhaps the most evocative story of the World Tree is that of the Norse myth of Odin's sacrifice. Odin is said to have hung upside down from the World Tree called Yggdrasill, for nine nights without food or drink and he also pierced himself with his spear. He was seeking knowledge and wasn't afraid to go to extremes to receive it. There are three Norns, maiden seers who create the fates of humans and Odin had watched them from afar and envied their abilities. They each tended to three different wells at the base of Yggdrasill. One of the ways that they created fate was to carve the rune symbols/letters into the trunk of Yggdrasill. This would create effects in all of the worlds. While Odin was hanging, he was gazing directly into one of these wells, the well of Urd, the well of fate. At the point of his death and collapse, the runes began to reveal

themselves in the well and he was given knowledge of them and access to their powers. After this, he emerged with tremendous powers of healing, protection, strength in battle, power over the elements, and the ability to raise the dead. The runes are still in popular use today. Used primarily for divination and magic, they are said to contain within themselves strong potency.

Yggdrasill means 'Odin's stead' or horse. Odin is said to have ridden the tree. As we will explore later in the book, the World Tree is the point at which shamanic journeys and the different worlds are accessed and navigated. We can also think of the witch's broomstick or stang (a wooden pronged stick). These are also tools for magical flight.

Echoes of Odin's hanging are also present in the Tarot card of The Hanged Man. Some of the central meanings of this card are sacrifice and delving deep into the unconscious to gain wisdom.

There is a deep message to be taken from Odin's story. Sacrifice and proving one's worthiness is necessary before one is given knowledge and power. Think back to the last chapter and the examples of gruelling initiations and tests. On another occasion Odin sacrifices his right eye to receive more knowledge, also at Urd's well. Profound knowledge and power come at a cost.

The World Tree has its ancient roots steeped in shamanic cultures all over the world with many striking similarities. It is an image that has carried through history and different world religions up until the present time. The Tree of Life in Kabbalah, the Tree of Immortality in Islam, and in India Ashvatta whose roots grow up to heaven and branches grow downwards. Of course, we have the bible's story of Adam and Eve and the Tree of Knowledge with the serpent offering the fruit of knowledge, which precipitated the Fall. The presence of a serpent again ties back to the symbolism present in so many shamanic cultures.

Links with the World Tree, the spinal column, and Kundalini have also been made. Manly P. Hall, an occult scholar, is probably the most well-known proponent of this view. The Kundalini is a strong spiritual force that all of us have contained at the base of our spines. Yoga is the most well-known system that works to raise this energy up our spinal columns, eventually reaching the crown of our heads. This is said to raise our consciousness from a baser more primal way of being to a more enlightened one, perhaps closer to the Heavens. Interestingly, this energy is represented by a snake or serpent coiled at the base of our spines which is so often seen all over the world within World Tree imagery. A feathered or winged serpent is a common feature also in shamanic cultures. The most obvious being the Mexican Quetzalcoatl. This represents the realised and raised Kundalini energy leading to a higher state of consciousness.

There is a recurring myth in different shamanic cultures about a paradisiacal time on Earth when there was no separation between Divine and the spirit world and us. There were no shamans. Everyone could go to the spirit world since there were no barriers. Due to humanity's arrogance, this barrier was created.

Another aspect of the Norse myths which bring us back to the importance of trees is their story of how humans were created. We originated from trees; the first man Ask came from the Ash tree and the first woman Embla came from the Elm tree.

The Dakota Sioux musician and activist, Floyd Red Crow Westerman, said: 'Our DNA is made of the same DNA of a tree. The tree breathes what we exhale. When the tree exhales, we need what the tree exhales. So we have a common destiny with the tree.'

Let's begin so, like Odin, we may ride the World Tree!

CHAPTER 3

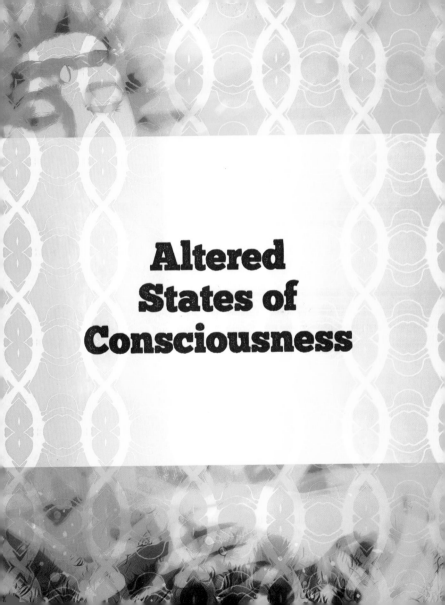

Altered States of Consciousness

Altered States of Consciousness (ASC), also known as shamanic trance and ecstatic trance, are central to shamanic practice. It is the magical ingredient that gives wings to shamanic flight. It is the means by which the journey into the realm of spirit can be taken. The way to cross through the veil between the physical and non-physical realms.

Extensive research has been done by neuroscientists over time to show how the different brainwave frequencies affect a person's states of consciousness. Brainwaves are measured in Hertz (Hz) just like in music:

BETA WAVES 13–30 HZ

This is the state where you are alert, focused and active. For instance, reading this! Any state where you need to concentrate to do something and for analytical thought. Stress and overthinking can occur in this state, but not necessarily.

ALPHA WAVES 8–13 HZ

This is a more relaxed state where you might daydream. Also called the hypnogogic state where you are falling asleep; it is between the sleeping and waking state. Some people describe this as the link between the conscious mind and the subconscious, and a gateway to meditation.

THETA WAVES 4–8 HZ

This is a deep trance state, where peak spiritual experiences can occur, and inspiration and creativity can be accessed. Also repressed emotions can surface

and be released. You could feel drowsy or aroused here. Rapid Eye Movement (REM), whilst asleep, also occurs here and we dream in this state. Very young children are in theta most of the time.

DELTA WAVES UP TO 4 HZ

This is a deep sleep state in which we aren't dreaming. Where the body can physically rejuvenate and repair itself. We can access non-physical states of reality here.

ASC or trance states are really a natural part of being human. Whether you are an experienced meditator, shamanic practitioner or complete novice at any of these experiences, you will have accessed these states at some point, even without considering it in these terms. For example, in different stages of sleep, dancing, going to a concert, a nightclub, intense exercise, during sex, singing or playing an instrument. I invite you to stop reading and recount in detail at least one of these experiences. What were you doing? How did it feel? Did you enjoy it? Was it at all frightening? Did your sense of time and your body change? You can write down your answers in a journal kept specifically for exploring your shamanic work.

These states are intensely liberating where we can switch from everyday thoughts, activities and feelings of being a separate individual to losing a sense of self, boundaries and control. This is more challenging for some than others, but practice makes perfect and it's good to experiment with different methods to see which ones suit you most.

The trance state can be two-fold in shamanic work. As mentioned, the shaman uses it to access information and travel in the spirit world, but equally the shaman can also play the drum or other instruments to put the recipient into trance because that state alone can be healing for them on all levels.

People who are not in the role of the shamanic healer can also use these states to facilitate their own healing, release and development. This reflects how far we have come with the use of different shamanic practices in modern times.

Music

REPETITIVE DRUMMING OR RATTLING

This is a feature in many shamanic cultures and has become a staple method in Core Shamanic journeying, either though live drumming or listening to recorded drumming. According to research by neuroscientists maintaining a beat of 205–220 bpm (beats per minute) for at least 15 minutes induces a trance state, sending the brainwaves into Theta. This state allows the practitioner to travel to different shamanic dimensions. In the last chapter the three worlds were mentioned. Those are the realms that we will be exploring through our journeys in this book.

The drum holds particular significance in indigenous cultures and is sometimes described as the heartbeat of the Earth. In the words of Black Elk from the perspective of the Oglala Sioux people: 'Since the drum is often the only instrument used in our sacred rites, I should perhaps tell you here why it is especially important and sacred to us. It is because the round form of the drum represents the whole universe, and its steady strong beat is the pulse, the heart, throbbing at the centre of the universe. It is the voice of Wakan Tanka (Great Spirit), and this sound stirs us and helps us to understand the mystery and power of all things.'

Rhythm itself, according to recent findings in neuroscience, is embedded in our bodies, minds, and consciousness. On the 22nd day in the womb a foetus jolts into life (this timing does vary between different foetuses). The first beat awakens nearby cells and they all synch in perfect rhythm to each other. These beating cells divide and become our heart. Perhaps, this explains the natural human instinct towards rhythm and the shared communal experience that transcends culture, class and other divisions.

So, let's sit for a while and feel our own rhythm/heartbeat...

Sit in a comfortable position. Close your eyes. Turn your attention inwards into the inside of your body. Into the

centre of your chest. Your heart. Feel your heartbeat. You might want to place your hands over your heart. Just sit for a while feeling, listening to the beat of your heart. As the beat of Mother Earth.

There is a plethora of other instruments used by shamanic cultures for ceremony and to induce trance, such as the didgeridoo, clap sticks, whistles, flutes, bells and the mouth harp. There is also, as mentioned above, the rattle, which can be used in much the same way as the drum. For the purposes of your own experiences you may want to try different instruments to see what you connect with more.

Singing

Singing is the other method of achieving trance states. For the Altaic shamans it was their mode of travelling up and down to the different worlds. For the Inuits, each shaman had their own particular song to invoke the spirits. In the Amazon vegetalistas (plant shamans) received specific songs from each plant spirit that they had worked with as an ally. These are called Icaros. Some shamans completely improvise their songs and due to their deep trance state don't remember it afterwards.

So singing is a powerful way to alter your state of consciousness, but it is more than that; it was also a means of invocation and communication with the spirit world. This is what the spirits recognise and understand.

This exercise is great to get you experiencing a sense of 'getting out of the rational mind' and its control. Thereby accessing ASC and a sense of greater fluidity. It can also lead to a feeling of well-being and emotional release.

OVERTONING

Also known as throat singing, overtoning is traditionally found in Mongolia, Siberia and parts of China. It has a very distinctive sound. With multiple tones being struck at the same time. There can be a whistling sound and with some a growling too! The tongue and mouth are used to split the sound like a sonic prism and an aural spectrum of rainbow colours are produced for those who can see energy. Siberian shamans say that they use overtoning to send away spirits that are causing problems to their clients as they dislike the resonance of overtoning.

Lyz Cooper, in her book *Sound healing*, writes, 'Over the last 20 years, every group in which I have presented toning and overtoning have said that overtoning creates a deeper ASC than toning. I believe this is due to the expanding nature of the harmonics, enabling consciousness to expand too.'

EXERCISE

Lyz Cooper, founder of the British Academy of Sound Therapy (BAST) has developed and taught a simpler way to access overtoning that is quicker to learn and easier on the vocal chords:

'Try toning in a fairly high pitch, moving from "EEE" to "OOO" and back again – listen for any whistling sounds.'

I also recommend that you start quietly for the first few minutes to warm up your voice. Exaggerate the shape of your mouth while making the sounds, but keep your tongue in the same place.

EXERCISE FOR ACCESSING YOUR UNTAMED SONG

◎ Find a comfortable seated or standing position.

◎ Close your eyes.

◎ Begin by humming or singing a single vowel tone (oo, ee, ah, for example)

◎ Gently warm up the voice.

◎ Allow your voice to go wherever it wants. Allow whatever sounds or tones to come out.

◎ Loud, quiet, melodic, monotone, beautiful, dissonant; try not to control it, just allow it.

Dance

Dance is one of the most fantastic mediums for reaching ecstatic states. It really allows the person to get out of their mind and into their body, and beyond the body into the spirit. Especially in modern society where office jobs and sedentary lifestyle are more commonplace. We can forget how to move and be fluid in our physicality. We can also use these trance dance states to access insights and to journey.

It is the most classical form of achieving trance from the point of view of indigenous shamanism. It is a way to journey in spirit and perform 'magical flight'. In Siberian and Chinese shamanism dancing accesses this and is a means to transform into a bird.

Piers Vitebsky talks about diagnosis by dance by Yakut Shamans in his book *The Shaman*: 'A Yakut shaman sets out dancing after a woman's sick soul by springing like his reindeer spirit mount and tapping himself with a stick as he goes. He dismounts, ties up his deer and continues on foot. Then he becomes a hawk, flies, and lands. Meanwhile his reindeer and the reindeer-vehicle of the evil spirit engage in battle, while the shaman slips off to check the condition of the patient's soul and dances his reaction to the state of the patient, whether curable or doomed.'

In some cultures, the shamans dance to bring on 'spirit possession'. This is prevalent in Haitian Vodou and in parts of Africa (where the spirits come to this world rather than the other way round), Mongolia, Siberia and Latin America. The spirits speak and act through the shaman.

The modern ecstatic dance movement is extremely popular now with different groups, events and classes appearing everywhere. Gabrielle Roth, with her 5 rhythms movement, was a huge influence on this. Many people became empowered through her work and inspiration:

'Shamanic healing is a journey. It involves stepping out of our habitual roles, our conventional scripts, and improvising a dancing path. The dancing path leads us from the inertia of sleepwalking to the ecstasy of living the spirit of the moment. Too often our lives get channelled into narrow, secure patterns, set into deadly routines. Some of us want out. Some of us want to let go and wake up to the power buried within us.'

If it is possible for you, I highly recommend that you find groups or classes to participate in a dance experience, since the power of dancing within a group is powerful and different to doing it at home or in a pair.

However, here are some exercises you can do at home. In terms of music, I recommend either repetitive shamanic drumming or unbroken music that has no lyrics and is fairly repetitive and non-obtrusive. There is plenty available online. Koshi music or hang drum music tracks that last for more than one hour are great. However, each person's needs and tastes will vary so have a look around for what works for you.

EXERCISE: BLINDFOLDED SHAMANIC TRANCE DANCE

This can be done with a partner to watch over you to make sure you don't bump into anything. Otherwise be mindful of your space, clear away furniture, objects and anything hanging that could interfere.

◎ Make an intention for your dance.
 Request an insight. Ask a question.

◎ Make your intention clear. Once you start to
   dance don't try to force an outcome. Allow it
   to come through the dance.

◎ Put on the blindfold or scarf over your eyes.

◎ Relax and let your body move you.

◎ Surrender to the experience.

◎ When you have finished, give thanks for
   whatever you received.

If you have company you may wish to discuss your experience
or you can write down in your journal what happened.

If relevant, let your partner dance while you look over
them. This can also be a good exercise for connection and
trust when done with another.

DANCE COMBINED WITH BODY ART/COSTUME

Shamanic dance was often connected to the spirits of animals. Whether this was for hunting purposes or in order to take on their qualities or powers whilst dancing. Costume, mask or bodypainting, sometimes with parts of the animal being worn, were frequently used in ceremony alongside the dancing. Shamans perceived that, during these dances, they transformed into the animal. The most famous of these being the 'bear dances' in North America and North Asia, where the shaman wore bear skin. This helps them to go even further out of themselves to become or embody the spirit of what it is that they are invoking.

It is possible that body art, costume and masks alone can produce ASC. When combined with dance, a truly powerful experience is possible. Ideally, a specific animal, quality (courage or gentleness, for example) or even an element from nature (fire, thunder etc.) is chosen. Body paint, masks, costumes, items of clothing, even simply specific colours or textures can be emphasised. You may find items that 'remind' you of what you are embodying. For instance, black clothes for crows or black panthers. Adapt it to your needs. You may want to create something extravagant or keep it very simple. Dancing in front of a mirror could enhance the experience especially if your face has been painted or covered, since you won't recognise yourself.

EXERCISE

◎ Choose the animal/quality/element that you want to dance.

◎ Invite the spirit of this to come into you during the dance.

◎ Put on music that you feel is suitable.

◎ Connect, dance and let it come to you through the dance.

◎ Observe how you feel embodying this.

◎ Feel what you can learn through muscle memory and body intelligence from this.

◎ When your dance is finished, thank whatever spirit has come to you.

◎ You might want to write down your experience in your journal or simply take some time to be quiet and integrate the experience.

◎ You may want to draw from the memory of this
experience to help you embody these qualities
in certain life situations or even repeat the
exercise again to use it as a source of personal
power or to cultivate particular qualities.

Dreaming

M any spiritual teachers now speak of the importance of positive thinking and how our thoughts create our reality, and there is some truth in this. However, a more shamanic perspective is that what we dream creates our reality. Mexican traditions teach that the dream state is energetically four times more powerful than the waking state. In Mexican traditions, the dream world is equated with the land of the dead.

Dreams are a huge part of shamanic traditions with some shamans receiving the majority of their training from spirits in the dream state.

This is another way to access the spirit world, communicate with spirit, and find out information. A shaman with highly developed dreaming skills can be completely lucid in the dream state; in other words, totally conscious that they are dreaming and able to carry out healing work for clients and even meet with other shamans and carry out work for the collective. Some have vast knowledge and understanding about dream interpretation.

Throughout this book, I will encourage you to explore your dream states to connect with spirit. Of course, not all dreams are profound spiritual experiences, some are simply the unconscious part of our brains processing memories and our emotional and mental states. However, it is

'We are what we dream.
Collective change begins with individual change.'
Sergio Magaña Ocelocoyotl

normally obvious when a dream has a more powerful significance – you can feel it. Or, for instance, you may wake up in the middle of the night at a time that is unusual for you; this can be your spirit's way of making sure you pay attention as there was a message in there for you. Remember to give thanks to the spirit world when you receive profound messages. They may see that as a sign that you are happy to receive more!

I would say that communicating with spirit through dreaming is much more profound than doing shamanic journeys with drumming. However, to become proficient in it takes a lot longer so it depends on how drawn you are to working with dreams and how much patience you have with that process. Some of you may have these gifts naturally. (Lucky you!) I have met people that lucid dream all night, every night, without any training.

TIPS TO START THE PROCESS
OF DEEPENING THE CONNECTION
WITH YOUR DREAM LIFE

◎ If you don't already have much recollection of your dreams, simply bringing your attention to them will bring you stronger recall.

◎ Get a book to use as a dream journal. You could use your shamanic journal for this purpose if you want to keep all your experiences together in one place.

◎ Before you sleep at night, have a clear intention that you will remember your dreams.

◎ Upon waking write whatever you can remember down. Even if you remember different dreams, if you don't write them down, the memories may vanish.

Sensory deprivation, fasting and sleep deprivation

These are very powerful ways to access trance states, but I won't speak at length about them as they are more extreme forms and would require the assistance of a trusted professional.

Darkness retreats were practiced by Taoists in caves as a way to develop stronger psychic abilities and deepened states of awareness as a lot of energy is used on everything that we take in visually. They would also combine this with fasting to further enhance the experience.

Fasting, sleep deprivation, dancing and drumming are all included in major ceremonies such as the Sun Dance and Moon Dance in the Americas. Sun being for men and moon being for women. People dance for days with very little sleep or food, sometimes until the point of collapse, inducing ecstatic flight.

Power plants

Peyote, cannabis, psilocybin mushrooms, salvia divinorum, iboga and ayahuasca, just to name a few, are a crucial part of some traditions. They induce intense altered states. Experiences of having direct communion with the spirit of these plants during ceremony is very common, with the plant teaching you much wisdom and guidance about your life and the nature of existence. Hence, they are also called 'Teacher Plants'. This is a big topic in itself, but I would say that if you feel a call to work with Teacher Plants then I suggest you find recommended plant shamans to work with as working with these plants can put you in a vulnerable position due to the heightened states that they produce so make sure you are in good hands.

CHAPTER 4

Tools, skills and ceremony

Tools

Some shamanic practitioners have loads of tools. I personally don't think this is important. The most important thing is to connect with whatever you are doing and to yield useful results. You may find with time that you have a mighty collection. Go with what works for you.

Here are some examples of what you might use:

✿ A drum, rattle or a form of musical instrument. You might find drumming downloads or CDs are enough for your journeys.

✿ Different types of incense or smudging sticks like sage, mugwort or copal and a heat-proof bowl for space-clearing (see pages 66-67) are very useful.

✿ A blindfold or scarf to cover the eyes during journeys and blindfolded dances.

✿ Notebook for keeping a dream journal, recording your journeys, or any other experiences you want to note down.

✿ A compass or compass app; this is helpful if you are planning to work with the directions.

☼ Some people love to work with crystals. They can be great amplifiers (quartz) or absorbers of energy (black stones).

Some tools will come from live beings; drumskins and feathers from animals or wood from trees on the frames of drums. Some of you will choose to work with tools that have not come from animals and there are many other options for drums. You can connect more deeply to your tools as shamanic allies by taking a journey to connect with the souls of your tools. We cover journeying on pages 73–79.

Shaman Aman Sirom performing ritual to appease the spirit of Akinabalu, the guardian of Mount Kinabalu in Malaysia.

Altars

Some people like to have an altar in your home or build one prior to doing any shamanic work. This is not a necessity but, again, see what works for you.

It can be a focal point to remind you of the sacred in your life and simply a beautiful way to honour different elements, totems, spirit guides, sacred objects and deities (if you work with any). It's an opportunity for creative expression and you may find that your altar changes with time depending on what is happening in your inner and outer life.

Altars are deeply personal, so follow your own way with this. However, if you are a person who thrives on structure you might want to consider looking at different models of the Medicine Wheel to inspire the placement of elements and other aspects on a classic altar. Something to represent each element is common practice. For example, a candle for fire, a cup for water, incense for air and a stone or crystal for earth. A stone or shell from a place that you consider sacred to you can be a way to remind or connect you to that place. Offerings for spirits, ancestors and deities can be put here too.

The Medicine Wheel

There are many versions of the Medicine Wheel. The most recognisable ones being from the Native North Americans. But there are other versions which may not be so obvious such as the Chinese Paqua and the Norse Aegishjalmur (Helmet of Awe). These wheels are markers of the cycles of nature. The cycle of the Sun, seasons, elements; think of it as a clock face. In Latin America they have dances where the four corners have different groups of dancers and they have a complex, ritualistic dance of the movement of all of these elements. Although, these wheels look static they are based on the movements of the natural cycles. In some traditions, each of the four quarters are a full stage of an initiation process.

The Paqua emphasises eight sides which can also be seen in nature on the pattern of a tortoise's shell. This wheel is used in Feng Shui, which can be used to map out how you arrange any space, such as your home or your workplace, to encourage a harmonious flow of energy.

The seven directions and their use in ceremony

T he seven directions can be called in and invoked to create a ceremonial space before you do any practice, whether a journey or a dance, for example. You are calling in different energies from nature, the elements, and they form a container for your work. As mentioned above there are differences in which elements and qualities embody each direction in each culture. I will make an invocation opposite, but this is just a suggestion based on my own training and just observations from nature. Feel free to study other systems and make adjustments according to your needs and, if you like sound, use a rattle or other instrument to play along with each part.

INVOCATION

(Face East)
**Calling in the Spirits of the East;
the Spirit of the rising sun, spring and new
beginnings. I welcome you into the space.**

(Face South)
**Calling in the Spirits of the South;
the Spirit of the Sun at its peak, the Summer and
full blooming. I welcome you into the space.**

(Face West)
**Calling in the Spirits of the West;
the Spirit of the setting Sun, the Autumn and of
shedding. I welcome you into the space.**

(Face North)
**Calling in the Spirits of the North;
the Spirit of the Night, the Winter and of our
Ancestors. I welcome you into the space.**

(Face Up)
**Calling in the Spirits of the Sky;
the Celestial bodies of the Sun, Moon, planet and**

stars. I welcome you into the space.

(Crouch down touching the Earth)
**Calling in the Spirit of the Earth below
our feet and down to your crystalline core
with all the abundance you bring.
I welcome you into the space.**

(Stand upright)
**Calling in and connecting with the Spirit of the
Centre. The place where all directions meet.
The Spirit of the present moment.
I welcome you into the space.**

◎ Feel these directions all meeting inside you and give
thanks.

◎ When you have finished your practice/ceremony, close the
space and send the energies back with gratitude, facing
each direction as you address them:

**Thank you, Spirit of the Centre
for your presence here.
I bid you farewell.**

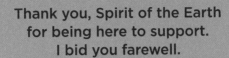

Thank you, Spirit of the Earth
for being here to support.
I bid you farewell.

Thank you, Spirits of the Sky
for your presence here.
I bid you farewell.

Thank you, Spirit of the North
and all of the Ancestors
for your presence here.
I bid you farewell.

Thank you, Spirits of the West
for your presence here.
I bid you farewell.

Thank you, Spirits of the South
for your presence here.
I bid you farewell.

Thank you, Spirits of the East
for your presence here.
I bid you farewell.

Keeping your space clear

When doing any shamanic work, it is important to keep the spaces that you work in 'clear' energetically. This can be as simple as opening the window beforehand to keep the air fresh and drawing the curtains to let light in. This helps with mental clarity and keeps the energy clear so we can be focused and feel that we are starting the work from a clean and clear place. Residual energies from other people or emotionally charged events can build up and become 'stuck' in a place. This can have

an effect on us whether we are working shamanically or even just carrying out our everyday tasks.

Traditionally, particular plants or incense are burned. These have special properties whose spirits clear the place up for us. Sage is very popular as a dried bundle that you light and emits a pungent smoke. Palo Santo, a sacred tree from Latin America, is also good for this purpose. It is a wood stick with a beautiful aroma. Copal and frankincense are incense resins that need to be burnt on charcoal discs. These plants also have anti-bacterial properties so they not only cleanse energetically but if there are air-born contagious bugs around they can prevent these from spreading. I tend to go around a room clockwise with the smoke making sure every corner has been covered. Corners are good spots for energy to get trapped. I open the window too if there is one so stuff can 'get out'.

We need to take some care with these plants as their popularity has risen and some of them have become overharvested so I suggest checking that your supplier is sourcing them ethically and check what your own country has available as sometimes there are plants that are less commercially popular but can link you more powerfully to your local traditions. Mugwort being a good example in the United Kingdom, for example, and pine in parts of the northern hemisphere.

Sound is also brilliant for breaking up and dispersing energies. Use your instruments, singing or even banging a saucepan will do the job!

On a very literal level, clean, dust and declutter a room.

Keeping yourself and others clear

T he smudge and incenses described on the previous page are also for purifying your own energy. We gather all sorts of energies from our activities, from others, from our thought forms. Especially now we are subjected to more and more electromagnetic frequencies (EMF) from the heavy use of technology. We can clear these to bring ourselves more fully into the present ready for the work. I use a feather to sweep the smoke through my aura starting above the head going all the way down to the feet, under the feet and between the legs, the hands and up the arms. If you are with another person you can take it in turns to sweep the smoke onto the back of each other.

A fantastic way to keep our energy clear is to spend time in nature, around trees and, if possible, do some wild swimming.

Grounding

With all of this journeying work and communion with spirits we really want to be as grounded in our bodies and to the Earth as possible. Shamanism is after all an Earth-based practice. It is easier for us to integrate the work and carry it out if we are more fully grounded. Shamanism is not about escaping the physical and our bodies; it's actually about going into the spirit realms to learn to enhance how we are living in the physical one on Earth. There is a reason after all why we have incarnated into a physical body.

The simplest way to do this is to walk barefoot outdoors, preferably on grass, a beach somewhere natural, but even walking barefoot on concrete will still be effective. Take a walk slowly, mindfully, feeling every single movement, every single part of your skin that is making contact with the ground. Take your time and breathe slowly and deeply.

A lot of research has been done on walking barefoot outdoors and it turns out that being barefoot allows us to conduct the Earth's electrons which are antioxidant in nature and can reduce inflammation. It can also improve sleep by normalizing circadian rhythms and can strengthen the immune system.

MEDITATION FOR GROUNDING

◉ Find a comfortable seated or standing position.

◎ Take a few moments to connect with your breath and feel yourself fully in your body.

◎ Bring your attention to your feet. Imagine, feel and see that you have tree roots growing out of the soles of your feet. Growing through the layers of earth, rock and crystal. Down and down into the molten core of Mother Earth.

◎ Feel that connection between your feet and the centre of the Earth.

◎ Breathing out of the soles of your feet, all the way down through your roots.

◎ Breathing back in from the centre of the Earth to the soles of your feet into your body.

◎ Continue this for some time. Feel yourself fill up with the Earth's energy.

◎ When you are ready, bring your awareness back to the room. You are rooted and grounded.

Chi Gong and Tai Chi as a shamanic practice

Chi Gong and Tai Chi have their roots in Chinese shamanic traditions and they are brilliant for training a person to be grounded and cultivate Chi (energy) in the lower Dan Tien centre. This is in the abdomen, our centre, and doing this gives us vitality, strength and takes our excessive energy out of our heads. I highly recommend these practices to anyone wishing to embark on shamanic work as it's a fantastic way to maintain your energy. There are hundreds of styles and practices so getting a good recommendation is ideal.

Shamanic journeying with drumming

This makes up a large part of practice for a lot of contemporary shamanic practitioners. This is just a description to give you an overview of journeying which we will actually go on to practice later in the book.

You will need a shamanic journey drum recording. These are available in many forms on the internet. Or you can purchase a CD from a spiritual website or shop. I recommend one with a call-back. This is where the rhythm changes so you know that it is time to complete the journey and prepare yourself to come back. The other option is for you to drum or rattle yourself. The rate of 205–220 bpm (beats per minute) is recommended.

Some people are happy with 15–20 minutes but others take longer. There are all sorts of varying times available. Once you begin your practice, you will get a sense of whether you are a fast or slow journeyer. See how much time you need to drop into it and adjust the length of your shamanic journeys accordingly. It may also depend on your intentions for your journey and how relaxed you are before you start.

Burning incense in the room can enhance the experience as some incenses create an altered state. Copal, frankincense and myrrh are great for this.

The key is to make a very clear intention before you start. Which world do you want to visit? Are you looking to connect with a specific guide? Do you have a specific area in which you need guidance or a specific healing that you are seeking? You might want to examine these questions before you do the journey to ensure as much clarity and clear results as possible. Journeys are a good way to find out if a place or spirit guide wants an offering and discovering what kind is appropriate.

In classical Core Shamanism you state the intention three times before starting. I think this is a good approach because it really focuses your intent for the journey.

You can also call in the directions or simply call in any helping spirits or ancestors you wish to be present. This gives your work protection and power.

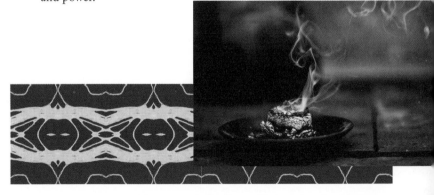

START THE JOURNEY

◎ Make yourself comfortable either seated or lying down using whatever you need, for example, a yoga mat, cushions and blankets.

◎ Have something to cover your eyes.

◎ Start the drumming recorded or live.

◎ State three times your intention for the journey.

◎ Begin your journey. This is a process of visualising where you are going and staying alert to signs, beings and imagery that comes to mind.

◎ When you hear the call-back, thank the spirits that you have been working with, say goodbye, and trace your steps back to where you started.

◎ Breath and make sure you feel all parts of you are fully in your body. If you feel they aren't, command them to come back and wiggle your toes and fingers and breathe yourself back into your body.

◎ When you are ready, open your eyes.

◎ If anything has been received during the journey – a gift that you can sense – you can shake a rattle (if you are using it) around your heart and whole body three times to integrate it. Otherwise, gently rub your solar plexus with the palm of your dominant hand.

I recommend that you make notes of your journey.

Integration and the aftermath

Taking a little time to be quiet to integrate and let everything settle into your body can be beneficial.

Doing a trance dance to physically embody and integrate the journey can also help to seal the work into ourselves.

Your journey may make perfect sense to you straight away but it also might not. Don't worry if it doesn't as sometimes things can take time to make sense to us. It is worth re-reading and revisiting at a later date. Certain elements might become clear or new things can arise.

NOTES ABOUT JOURNEYING

Journeying is an amazing and fantastic thing, but it can take time for some people to feel that they are making a connection. Don't worry at all if you practice journeying and feel that nothing or very little has happened.

Don't give up and try not to get stressed about it as this won't help. An attitude of determination with non-attachment will probably yield the best results.

Some people are also less visual. Some hear, feel sensations, or even just a sense of knowing. Some lucky people have all of these things! It's worth remembering that you may not receive purely through vision.

Sometimes it can also be the case that more is happening than we realise. Simply the vibrations of the drums are very healing for us on all levels and journeys to the Lower World take us to a place of rest and recuperation. Don't underestimate your experience because you didn't have the full fireworks. Also, if sharing experiences with others, try not to compare. Your journeys are very personal and you may receive something incredibly simple, but this could hold precious value and power.

If you feel that you really don't resonate so much with journeying then other methods may be better for you. This could be dreaming, seeing signs in the outside natural world, or perhaps dance. It's about finding your own way.

CHAPTER 5

The Lower World:
power animals

Let's begin to explore the three shamanic worlds – the Lower, Middle and Upper worlds. The three-world model is commonplace in contemporary shamanism and gives us a simple framework to work with here.

All three worlds are within the World Tree and the Lower World is underneath the tree. It is often seen as a beautiful, bountiful place of nature. When we take a journey there we start at the base of the World Tree and we find a way to go down underneath the ground. Picture a well, a hole, a shoot, a ladder or steps and start to descend. In the Norse tradition it is called 'Hel' and yes this is where the Christian 'Hell' came

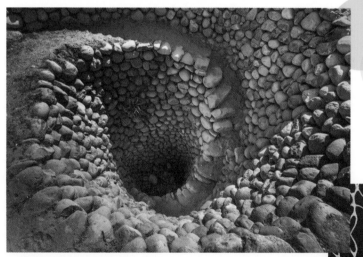

Visualise a hole in the ground or a ladder that you can descend in order to reach the Lower World. You can also climb down the roots of the World Tree.

from. But in the shamanic view, it is not a place of punishment or where evil resides. This place is where we often connect with power animals and animal spirit helpers. It is a place of profound healing. It is also the place of our ancestors and of the dead, and a place to explore our shadow aspects (parts of ourselves we have repressed and don't want to acknowledge). Soul parts that have become split-off from us during stressful or traumatic events are also found here. Soul retrieval is a very common part of shamanic practitioner's work and they often journey here to find these parts and re-integrate them back into the client. On a more abstract level we can retrieve power or qualities that we have disconnected from.

The shamanic concept of power

When speaking about the power of a shamanic practitioner, it is about their ability to be effective. It speaks of their ability to create healing results, go into trance and to receive the necessary information. A shaman does not do this alone; they have a team of spirit guides and allies working with them.

Another more contemporary view is that power comes from living by what your true heart's desires and passions are. It means not 'giving away your power' to family, colleagues, peers and partners by allowing your behaviour and life choices to be affected by pressure and expectations. This can lead to problems on all levels, including physical health. This is because you have allowed your power to 'leak out'. An example would be if I wanted to become an artist and this was a strong natural desire and my parents put a heavy amount of psychological pressure on to me to become a doctor. If I gave in to that pressure out of fear of displeasing them then this could eventually lead to me having health problems or emotional issues.

Power is also about a sense of healthy boundaries in relationships. These are the sort of factors that a practitioner who works with clients will be working with. In the case of this book, where this is solo work aimed at being an introduction to shamanic work, we can look and enquire within with these practices to explore these issues, but may need the help of an experienced practitioner further down the line to resolve them.

Power animals

To begin any kind of shamanic work we need to connect with spirit guides. This is how we begin to build up our own power within this work. We all have a spirit animal intrinsically connected to us. In European traditions this is called our 'fetch', a personal spirit helper that is usually an animal. By connecting to, and building a relationship with, your power animal, you both grow in strength and power. It is also available for guidance and it embodies qualities that you can draw on, particularly in times when you need it. This animal is always with you. It is a part of you. For anyone who has read it, think of the daemons in the Phillip Pullman trilogy *His Dark Materials*, where each character had an animal attached to them and was always with them. In some traditional shamanic communities, the apprentice would search for their animal spirit in a vision quest, going out into the wild for days until they receive the correct signs from nature and the spirit of the animal. Sometimes we have more than one animal helper that is with us for our lifetime, but we can only have one fetch.

There are also animal spirit helpers that are with us temporarily to aid and guide us or to deliver a message during particular times in our lives. Each animal has its own 'medicine', abilities and powers that we can take on and into us. For instance, during a very challenging period, you may need the warrior spirit of a bear or, during a time where many things are hidden, owl can assist you to reveal them. We can learn a lot from looking up their natural habits. Are they solitary? Are they nocturnal? How do they hunt or are they hunted? What is their place in the eco-system? Are they confrontational? What are their mating habits? This information can give us a lot of wisdom around how to approach different situations in our lives. For instance, the qualities of an eagle might be perfect for one person but an ant's might be more suitable for another.

Have a think about particular animals to which you feel drawn. They may or may not be your personal animal spirits but there are qualities they have that attract you.

Remember also if there are certain animals that have been present in your dream life at different times in your life.

Are there animals that frighten you? There could be a message there for you.

It's best to keep an open mind when beginning your connection to animal spirits. Your animal guide might not be what you expect. They also each have unique powers. Don't be fooled by appearances and think that only the most ferocious and beautiful animal is powerful. A termite is incredibly powerful but not one we would immediately think of.

There is a lot of information online and in books around animal spirits and what they can mean. This can be very interesting, but I would recommend working in direct communication with your guide to learn from it directly beforehand. There are some wonderful myths in different cultures around animals that are worth looking into once you've made that initial bond.

The relationship with the animal spirit, particularly your personal one, will build with time. If this is the first time connecting to it you may just want to enjoy each other's company, like when you meet a new friend. Then you can ask questions and your animal spirit can impart teaching over time.

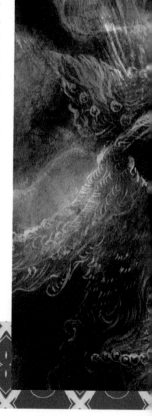

JOURNEY TO THE LOWER WORLD TO MEET AN ANIMAL GUIDE

State your intention three times for your journey:

I am journeying to the Lower World to meet my power animal

Or

I am journeying to the Lower World to meet an animal guide that will help me with... (e.g. finding a new home, finishing my degree)

◎ Make your way down to the Lower World until you reach a cave-like place.

◎ Walk through this cave until you come into an opening which is the Lower World.

◎ Here you will find your power animal.

◎ Sometimes more than one animal can appear so just ask it four times 'are you my power animal?' until you are given clear confirmation.

◎ You may just want to spend time bonding with it. Playing, dancing, see whatever arises. Especially in the initial contact.

◎ If you want to ask questions, go ahead.

◎ Enjoy your time until you hear the drumming change, then prepare to come back.

◎ If this is your first time connecting with an animal put your arm out above your heart (in the physical realm) and bring the animal into your heart.

◎ Give thanks to the spirit and for the journey.

◎ Come back into your body, making sure you feel fully grounded and 'in your body'.

◎ If you have a rattle, it's good to shake the rattle around your heart and your whole body three times to integrate the new energy.

◎ Have some quiet time to integrate the experience. Write down your journey in your journal.

Animal encounter

Joseph is a seasoned shamanic journeyer but he never felt that he had made that connection with his power animal or fetch. So his intention was to meet it, if he hadn't already, but at least to get some clarification.

'I saw flashes of chameleon, squirrel, lion, elephant, salmon, octopus… and then landed on jaguar. I saw the earth/mud move to become a jaguar pattern, almost the spirit of the Earth embodied. It climbs trees, swims in swamps and is happy to adapt to all terrains. Confident, strong, it showed me its muscles.'

OTHER WAYS TO CONNECT WITH ANIMAL GUIDES

There are alternative ways to connect with animal guides – in dreams, for example. You can ask for a dream to connect you with your power animal before you go to sleep. If it doesn't happen that night, you can persist until it does.

Asking for outer signs can be quite revealing about the thin veil of reality that we live in. If you live in an environment that is urban without much wildlife, these signs can come to you in interesting forms such as adverts, objects and gifts.

Otherwise ask for nature herself to reveal the animal to you in the flesh. If you receive such a blessing, be sure to give thanks in the form of prayers and perhaps physical offerings.

Observe how the animal behaves. Which direction does it appear from? Which direction does it go to (if it's moving)?

During the writing of this book a raven appeared to me. It's one of my primary animal guides. I have never seen a wild one in London before. I was in central London in quite a busy area and it flew down and sat on a post right next to me for a minute. I was quite taken aback! Sometimes they can appear when it's least expected.

POWER RETRIEVAL JOURNEY

Here you are going to receive a gift of power in the form of an object, symbol, words or an animal. You could be searching for power in a specific form e.g. creativity, intelligence, courage, joy, productivity. This can be something you feel you've lost touch with. Or you can just request the form of power that you need most right now and see what comes. You might find that a narrative is revealed to you about why this has been lost or how to maintain it or you might simply receive what you need with no explanation.

State your intention three times for the journey:

I am journeying to the Lower World to retrieve power

or

I am journeying to the Lower Word to retrieve power and healing for any loss of (courage/joy/vitality etc.)

◎ Make your way down to the Lower World until you reach a cave-like place.

◎ Walk through this cave until you come into an opening which is the Lower World.

◎ Meet with your power animal there to assist and protect you on this journey.

◎ You may be taken on a journey to show you what has happened to you. Be open-minded as you go with it.

◎ You will be given the appropriate symbol, animal or words.

◎ There may even be instructions on how to utilise this in the physical realm or you can simply integrate it and take this with you.

◎ When you hear the drum change, prepare to come back, remembering to thank the spirits for the journey.

◎ Put your arms out above your heart (physically) and bring whatever you have received into your heart.

◎ Give thanks to the spirit and for the journey.

◎ Come back into your body, making sure you feel fully grounded and 'in your body'.

◎ If you have a rattle, it's good to shake the rattle around your heart and your whole body three times to integrate the new energy.

◎ Have some quiet time to integrate the experience. Write down your journey in your journal.

MOTIVATION RETRIEVAL JOURNEY

Lily had many fantastic ideas but when it came to being productive with her time and motivated into action she seemed to have resistance so she did a motivation retrieval journey.

'I got taken to many scenes at different times in my life. Seeing clothes that I'd forgotten about. A time where I saw a spirit and became very scared. An idealised image of how I'd imagined myself in the future when I was 17 that I'd lost any hope of becoming. A time in an emotionally abusive relationship in my twenties where I had taken on the belief that I had nothing to offer the world and my life was over.

'I was given a bag of powder and a younger version of me came into me. I was quite taken aback by the intensity of where this issue had come from.'

This sounds as though Lily also experienced a soul retrieval, which is usually done with the assistance of a healer but sometimes spirit will heal you without any healer's intervention.

JOURNEY FOR PHYSICAL HEALING

State your intention three times for your journey:

I am journeying to the Lower World to heal my (right shoulder/asthma/ headaches etc.)

◉ Make your way down to the Lower World until you reach a cave-like place.

◉ Walk through this cave until you come into an opening which is the Lower World.

◉ Here meet with your power animal to assist and protect you on your journey.

◉ Let the journey unfold. You may receive further information about actions you need to take in the physical world afterwards. Or why it happened. Be open to whatever arises.

◉ Enjoy your time until you hear the drumming change, then prepare to come back.

◎ Give thanks to the helping spirits and for the healing and the journey.

◎ Come back into your body, making sure you feel fully grounded and 'in your body'.

◎ If something was given to you or placed into you then it's good to shake the rattle around your heart and your whole body three times to integrate it.

◎ Have some quiet time to integrate the experience. Write down your journey in your journal.

CHAPTER 6

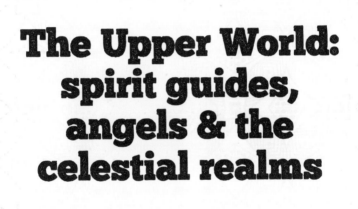

The Upper World: spirit guides, angels & the celestial realms

The Upper World is the realm of the skies. The realm of spirit guides, angels, ascended masters, deities and the stars. In Norse it is called Asgard or 'Fortress of the Celestial Gods'. This is where we go to contact our spirit guides. The information and guidance we get is of a more spiritual nature, a bigger picture perspective, wisdom for healing and guidance. Many of the beings here will be interested in the higher evolution of us humans and want to guide us towards a higher consciousness. There is a light and airy atmosphere in this world and it feels more 'ethereal'.

I myself experience it as being wide open landscapes, forests full of snow-covered trees, castles and magical caves. The Yakut shamans also found the Upper World to be cold and on returning from journeys there would sometimes be covered in icicles. But, as with all of your explorations, be open to whatever your personal experiences are.

The Ancients clearly had a profound relationship with the Cosmos. There are many stories about cultures having directly descended from Sky Beings. The Hopi people say that their ancestors called the Chuhukon originate from the Pleiades. Stories abound of Sky Beings coming down to Earth to teach certain cultures or tribes their knowledge.

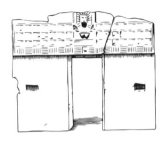

Many sacred sites around the world were built in alignment with the star constellation of Orion, but without the use of telescopes and the kind of technology we have now. Perhaps shamanic communion with the Upper World gave them this knowledge and connection?

There are special sites all over the world that are considered to be 'Stargates', portals to certain star constellations where humans can access them or Sky Beings can come to us. Some people have taken this idea very literally! I would imagine that these spectacular places facilitate an express route for journeying into these Upper World star realms. Many shamanic and spiritual practitioners visit them for this very reason to access these other dimensions more easily. Some examples are Stonehenge, Tiahuanaco in Bolivia called 'Gate of the Sun', and Abydos in Egypt.

JOURNEY TO THE UPPER WORLD

State your intention three times:

**I am going to the Upper World
to meet my spirit guide**

Or

**I am going to the Upper World
to ask my spirit guide for guidance
about...**(explicitly state what it is that
you need to know)

◎ See yourself at the World Tree then climb up the tree. If
your animal guide is a winged one let it fly you up there.

◎ Go to the top of the tree and fly up into the sky. You may
find yourself hitting a paper-like membrane. If there's no
hole in it, just pierce it and fly through.

◎ Here you are in the Upper World.

◎ With your intention keep moving until you reach a place where your guide is waiting for you.

◎ Get to know each other. If you have a particular question, ask it. See what arises.

◎ When the drum call-back comes, prepare to come back.

◎ If you have been given something during the journey then physically reach your arms up above your heart and pull it into your heart.

◎ Give thanks to the spirit and for the journey.

◎ Come back into your body, making sure you feel fully grounded and 'in your body'.

◎ If you have a rattle, it's good to shake the rattle around your heart and your whole body three times to integrate the new energy (if you received something).

◎ Have some quiet time to integrate the experience. Write down the journey in your journal.

UPPER WORLD ENCOUNTER WITH ODIN

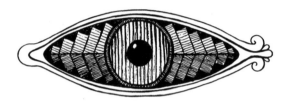

I was met with my wizard guide who took me to Odin who looked like a gigantic statue. Odin asked me to look into each of his eyes and tell me what I saw.

I looked into the eye socket of the sacrificed eye and saw a bottomless black void so I said, 'the void'. In the other one I saw star light. I said, 'Infinite possibility'. He said, 'choose one.' I chose infinite possibility.

I felt my arms being torn off and he gave me a raven. Then I saw the face of someone I had met a few months ago. He said that he could teach me more about Norse shamanism.

I lost consciousness for a short time then saw that my range of vision was completely covered by a bear skin. I realised it was for me and he said, 'You'll be stronger now.'

CHAPTER 7

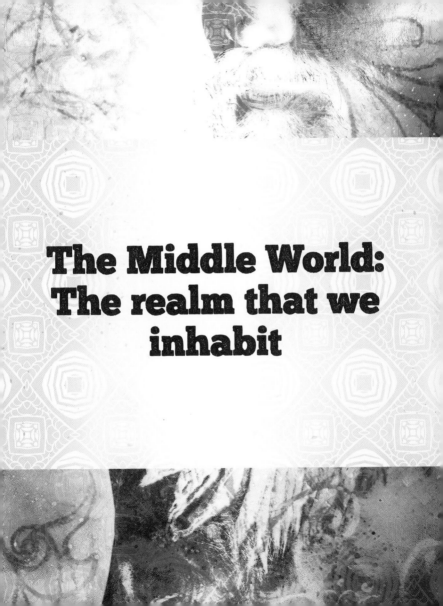

The Middle World: The realm that we inhabit

The Middle World is the world that we live in. The physical side – our bodies, objects, places, any feature in nature (the trees, rocks, flowers) and other living beings. It is also the energetic side of our reality. Discarnate spirits that did not find their way into the Underworld after physical death.

In Norse this would be Midgard and for any Tolkien fans, yes, this is a literal reference to 'Middle Earth'.

This can be a challenging realm to work in because there are so many lost spirits wandering around. When you work here, you need to take care not to let anything that isn't relevant to your journey intervene. Stay focused on what you have gone there for. Also, extra power and protection is advised so there'll be an exercise overleaf on how to acquire a protective guide in the form of an animal helper to be with you for any journeys you do here. This is the realm where psychopomp work is done; psychopomp is a term meaning one who assists lost souls to get to the Underworld.

I recommend that you develop and gain confidence in your journeying abilities in the Lower and Upper World first and establish a solid relationship with at least your primary animal spirit. This is why I have put the Middle World last in the list. You will have a good grounding and have acquired some shamanic power with your animal spirit.

There is quite an infinite potential of work that can be done here. You can visit the spirit of places, a company, a community, animals and even planets. Manifestation is possible. If you were looking for a job, you could connect with the spirit of the job that is your best outcome and call it to you. Ask what's needed to attain it. Visit the spirit of your home or workplace to find out what space-clearing it needs or how it can be arranged more harmoniously. Journey to the spirit of plants and minerals to learn more about them. This is really a huge arena for divination work. Divination meaning 'to be inspired by God'. Here you can receive guidance, information and even prophecies.

In Iceland it is well known that roads and buildings are only built after the local shaman has consulted the spirits of the place to see if they have permission of the land and the resident elemental spirits. Sometimes they get told 'no' and they respect this. Places may also require offerings so we can find out this sort of information in these journeys.

When journeying to the Middle World, you will require more protective power and you can find this by calling in your animal guides to help you.

JOURNEY TO THE MIDDLE WORLD TO MEET WITH A PROTECTIVE MIDDLE WORLD GUIDE

State your intention three times:

**I am going to the Middle World
to meet my protective
Middle World guide.**

◎ See yourself at the World Tree, then go behind the tree. I go via a wall that I run through, but others see a forest that you can go through. The transition is fast as it's on our level.

◎ See yourself in a clearing and your Middle World animal guide will be there.

◎ Any uncertainty, just ask it four times for confirmation that it is your Middle World guide.

◎ Get to know each other. You might go exploring together in the Middle World. See what arises.

- ◎ When the drum call-back comes, prepare to come back.

- ◎ If this is the first time connecting with an animal put your arm out physically above your heart and bring the animal into your heart.

- ◎ Give thanks to the spirit and for the journey.

- ◎ Come back into your body, making sure you feel fully grounded and 'in your body'.

- ◎ If you have a rattle, it's good to shake the rattle around your heart and your whole body three times to integrate the new energy.

- ◎ Have some quiet time to integrate the experience. Write down the journey in your journal.

JOURNEY TO THE MIDDLE WORLD FOR WHAT YOU WANT TO EXPLORE

This can be a wide range of things. The spirit of the company you work in or a project or creation you have in mind. The spirit of your home, workplace or any particular place you are thinking of living or working in to check if it's right for you and others. The spirit of your family to see where harmony is needed. The spirit of a pet, plant or stone to be able to communicate more clearly.

State your intention three times for the journey.

I am journeying the Middle World to make contact with my (home/company/pet) **for information on how to create harmony and solve problems.**

◎ See yourself at the World Tree, then go behind the tree. Use the same method as earlier (page 112). The transition is fast as it's on our level.

◎ See yourself in a clearing and your Middle World animal guide will be there to assist and protect.

◎ Together find the spirit of what you've come to meet.

◎ Ask whatever questions you need to. See if they want to convey anything else to you.

◎ When the drum call-back comes, prepare to come back.

◎ If this is the first time connecting with a particular animal that you have met, put your arm out physically above your heart and bring the animal into your heart.

◎ Give thanks to the spirit and for the journey.

◎ Come back into your body, making sure you feel fully grounded and 'in your body'.

◎ Have some quiet time to integrate the experience. Write down the journey in your journal.

MIDDLE WORLD JOURNEY TO MEET WITH THE SPIRIT OF A PROJECT

Joseph was about to collaborate with a friend on a music performance and wanted guidance on it so he met the project's spirit in the Middle World.

'I saw the spirit of the co-creator on my project and saw her as an African tribeswoman with a spear. She projected such a strong positive force. I felt into her essence and saw she was a pioneering force.

'Jaguar led me around the project, to the creation, rehearsal, recording and delivery of it and I saw some of the costumes.

'Jaguar and I sat on the moon looking back at the Earth giving a sense of "the Overview Effect". It reminded me of when humankind first looked back objectively at our planet and the effect that had on our thinking.'

CHAPTER 8

Empowering places and what grows within them

Were we to approach shamanism in a way that was much less about any tradition or system and more personal, then connecting to your surroundings would be a paramount way to work shamanically.

A primary aspect of shamanism is the connection to nature, land and the spirits that inhabit them. This strongly roots you and connects you to where you live and gives you a deeper understanding and communion with your surroundings. Many of us have lost this connection, not viewing our location as a living, breathing being, made up of many spirits. This is not only true of natural places, but also of the urban sprawl.

To give myself as an example, I live in London. We have the river Thames, who is a powerful and beautiful spirit. There are also hills, parks, other bodies of water, trees… wherever you live there will be many features to choose from. I know there may be some of you who live a nomadic lifestyle, but perhaps you have places you are in regularly or simply places that are close to your heart. If you spend a lot of time on aeroplanes or boats, you could choose to connect with sky spirits or the ocean that you regularly are in.

SIMPLE EXERCISE TO CONNECT WITH A PLACE

If this place is accessible to you and you can be there without being disturbed, then take some time to be there and go into a meditative state. Slow your thoughts, your mind and your breathing and really tune into and connect with this place. Ask to make an authentic connection. Just be there, feel, and observe. Notice anything that happens while you are doing this. It could be the elements – wind, rain, clouds, the sun – or animal and human activity. It could be certain sounds. See whatever comes up during this process. When you feel it is the right time, give thanks to the spirits of the place. You might want to write down the experience if anything came up for you or if you felt some sort of message. It may be that you just felt a simple connection.

I also recommend taking a Middle World journey (pages 114–115) to make this connection.

MIDDLE WORLD JOURNEY ENCOUNTER OF THE RIVER THAMES

The Thames appeared to me as a blue lady with a powerful, regal personality. She spoke about how the Romans built London as they recognised that her presence would make a good site for a city. She said that London's power comes from her and she protects the city. She said she had another name before she was called the Thames. I have since checked and she was called 'Tamesas' and 'Tamesis'. She advised me to take boat trips on her to connect more with her. She asked me to bring her waters from the sacred sites that I visit.

Connecting with local plants

Connecting with plants on a spiritual level is a wonderful experience. Due to industrialization, many people have lost connection with our local and seasonal plants since we can have access to so many fruits and vegetables at all times of year from all over the world. Connecting with our local plants, not necessarily for consumption, can give us a deeper sense of the natural spirits around us. Plants hold powerful healing qualities and wisdom.

I would suggest doing an exercise very similar to the one to connect to a place (page 121). Think about where you would like to do it or you literally might want to walk out of your front door and see where your feet take you. Perhaps a park? Even in the city there can be a surprising amount of plants. Go with your feeling. But have the intention that this will be a plant that you will benefit from connecting with right now.

VISION WALK TO CONNECT WITH A PLANT ALLY

Decide where you would like to take this walk.

Before starting state your intention clearly to yourself:

I am going on a vision walk to connect with a plant ally that is relevant to me now.

◎ Take a moment to put yourself into a meditative state or slightly altered state. Slow down your breathing, turn your attention inwards and towards your intention.

◎ Begin your walk.

◎ Allow yourself to be led as if an intuitive inner compass was guiding you.

◎ This process could be very quick or could take some time.

◎ Have absolute trust in your intuition that you know when you have found the plant.

◎ When you have found the plant, respectfully ask if you can take a small piece of it with you.

◎ Remove the piece, there may be some loose that you can take. Flower, leaf, twig, seed, flake of bark. If possible, take more than one part as each part will show you something different. Be careful not to take so much as to damage the plant at all.

◎ Give thanks.

◎ Spend some time looking at the plant itself and what you have taken, noting the shape, colours, textures, smell. Is it rough, sturdy or delicate? Get as much detail as you can.

◎ From your observations, do you have any ideas about what it's good for?

◎ You can sleep with the plant under your pillow or next to you as you sleep. Ask it to connect with you in the dream state.

◎ Next thing would be to take a journey to it to meet with its spirit and commune in another way.

Plant ally found

I did the exercise on pages 124–125 in the mountains in the South of Spain. But my vision walk was very brief. I stepped out of the room outdoors and right in front of me was a weedy bush with beautiful magenta flowers. My rational mind tried to kick in telling me it couldn't be that easy, but I knew that this was it! I took a flower, thanking the plant. It felt very feminine, sensual, maybe an aphrodisiac, and I felt euphoria coming from it. It had a beautiful scent and was a night bloomer so smelt stronger in the night-time. I put it in a glass of water overnight and slept with it next to my head. The water tasted beautiful in the morning. I asked my friend who lives in the area if she knew it. She said, 'Yes that's Dama de la Noche. It's a weed; it grows everywhere.'

Dama de la noche means 'lady of the night'.

NB: Do not ingest any plant unless you are aware of what it is and that it is not toxic to humans.

Power places

There are thousands of sites all over the planet that the ancients considered to be power places. Some are built by humans such as pyramid sites, for example Giza in Egypt and Teotihuacan and Chichen Itza in Mexico. Some are standing stones such as Stonehenge and Avebury in England and Carnac in France. Others are sacred wells, for example, the white and red spring in Glastonbury in England and the many thousands of sacred wells all over Ireland. There are also natural power places with no man-made construction such as Uluru in Australia, the Vortexes in the

Sedona desert in the USA, and Sacred Mijakenda Kaya forest in Kenya.

These places are considered to hold strong spiritual power and are sometimes seen as portals between the spirit world and our world. Subsequently they have often been used for ritual and ceremony.

A shamanic tree at Olkhon Island on the Baikal lake in Russia.

Ley lines

Ley lines, also known as Holy Lines and Dragon Lines, are a relatively new concept that were put forward to the public first by William Henry Black in 1870 and Alfred Watkins in 1920. They were likened to the Earth's meridian lines (humans have energetic meridian lines that are worked on by acupuncturists) and that they form a grid or matrix around the Earth. There are also theories that they are formed by underground streams and magnetic currents. They are said to contain a strong current of the Earth's energy. These were seen to be crossing over at major sacred sites such as Stonehenge, Machu Picchu and the pyramids of Giza. They pinpoint a concentrated area of energy, explaining why these particular sites were chosen. Ley lines are a controversial topic; many argue they can't be measured scientifically while others claim they can through dowsing.

Visiting power places

The magnetism of power places is unmistakable. Think of the thousands of people that have no interest in spirituality who flock to visit these sites. Coaches of people turning up at the major sites hourly, almost daily, all year.

Shamanic and spiritual practitioners can feel a great pull to come to these sites as they can have enhanced experiences and shifts to what they may experience otherwise. It is good to acknowledge and respect the site and introduce yourself upon entering. This doesn't have to be formal, but it's like going into someone's home. You can take a pause, have a sense of saying hello, and introducing yourself before entering. This can be done silently if you prefer.

If you know someone that has worked with a site and is familiar with it, then this can be great. It is like having a spiritual tour guide since the spirits of the place can get to know you and vice versa. The spirits may open up more quickly for you. However, of course this isn't always possible. It's good to be aware that these sites can hold very powerful energies and not to make anyone fearful, but it's worth having a healthy respect for this. There are also routes to take around the sites that are more beneficial. Many of these sites are designed to be used in a specific way that may have been forgotten with time. I've had the privilege to be taken around sites in Mexico on trips with Sergio Magaña. He taught us about this, particularly with the site Teotihuacan. He said because of the way access has been laid out, many people start with the pyramid of the Sun or the Quetzacoatl temple and finish on the Moon and, as a result, they leave with a headache. That is because ideally you start at the Moon temple, since this is where you shed any heavy energy. The you go to the Sun temple to strengthen your connection to fulfilling your greatest destiny. Then the Quetzacoatl temple assists you to raise your energy to become enlightened.

If you don't have access to a guide or any knowledge, then I recommend taking a Middle World journey to a site first to learn about it and make an introduction or ask to connect in the dream state. You may receive amazing information. Call upon your animal guides, spirit guides and ancestors for extra protection. If you are blessed with strong intuition or reception of guidance in the moment, then this is a great place to utilise those abilities.

Sacred water from Holy Wells

The average adult is made up of 50–65% water and 71% of the Earth is covered in water, so water is very important. Dr Masaro Emoto was the late Japanese scientist who brought the concept that water is a living consciousness that can be programmed and affected by its environment to a mainstream audience. Shamanic cultures have always understood this view of water as a sacred source of life. Many wells have been sites for pilgrimage and some are said to have water with curative properties. This water will already have a spiritual charge from the potency of the place but there are often higher contents of certain minerals depending on the well. For example, the red spring in Glastonbury is called red because it has a residual copper-red colour because of its high iron content. The white spring has high calcite content.

If you have the opportunity to visit one of these amazing places then I recommend making the most of this and further charge any water that you collect with intent and blessings. *This can also be applied to any water, including tap water.* As all water carries intent and prayers. Ideally collect the water in a glass bottle.

BLESSING AND CHARGING WATER WITH INTENT

◎ Place the water in its receptacle between your hands.

◎ Speak into the water giving thanks to the place that it has come to you from.

◎ Thank the spirit inside the water.

◎ Tell it you love it.

◎ Ask for any healing you would like or qualities you want to infuse it with; see them clearly in your mind's eye and blow that intention into the water three times.

◎ Before drinking it or using it, hold it between your hands and offer it to the seven directions.

◎ Enjoy!

This water can be drunk, cooked with, poured into a bath (even a small amount will affect the vibration of all the bath water) or a little kept on your altar. You can also use a small amount to cleanse an area in your body that needs healing or rub a little on your third eye to help it open more.

CHAPTER 9

Death and the Ancestors

Training in preparation for death

D eath is a theme of huge importance in shamanic traditions as it is the ultimate journey into the spirit realms since there is no body to which you can return. In some cultures, a large part of spiritual training is devoted to learning how to die. Lucid dreaming is a key practice since when dying, many lose consciousness to what is happening. Books such as the Egyptian Book of the Dead were designed to be guides to warn people about the different realms, demons and tests to be faced after dying to prepare for them. There were also rites to be read out for the deceased to give them protection on their journey.

Another message beyond simply being ready for death and not becoming lost during the transition was to also become more conscious and lucid in day-to-day life and maximise your life in the here and now.

This kind of training is quite extensive and is a path and a commitment of its own, so I would recommend finding a teacher to learn this with if this is calling you. But, for now, strengthening your connection with your dream life and the land of the dreaming (which is also the land of the dead), as with the recommendations and exercises given throughout the book is a good place to begin.

Grieving and our ancestors

Something that has created many problems in our societies in the West has been our repression of true grieving and honouring of our ancestors. Grieving, of course, is a deeply personal and unpredictable process. One of the things that unites us as human beings is the experience of loss. Shamanic cultures have a lot to teach us that can help us to process our pain.

I myself am of mixed heritage (British and Chinese) and have witnessed the contrast between the two cultures when it comes to death. I have felt that many funerals that I've attended in the UK give the participants little time and attendees, apart from close family, rarely shed tears. On my mother's side they celebrate yearly the festival of Ching Ming (also known as Tomb Sweeping Day), which is at the beginning of Spring. Food, drink, incense, hell money, and gifts are given. And, as the title suggests, time is taken to clear away the overgrown weeds on the tombs.

When my grandmother passed away, sadly I couldn't make her funeral in Malaysia. She had a three-day ceremony with Buddhist, Confucian, and Taoist rites. People cry and they have three full days to really express their grief.

It is important for us to fully honour our grief and really let it out and share it collectively with the community. Sometimes it is not only the grief for that person, but built up grief from other losses. This process of grief is not only important for us, but it is necessary for the deceased to feel fully honoured so they can move forward in peace. Malidoma Patrice Some from the African Dagara tribe works extensively with teaching Westerners to reclaim this lost connection. He writes: 'Only by passionate expression can loss be tamed and assimilated into a form that one can live with. The Dagara also believe that the dead have a right to collect their fair share of tears. A spirit who is not passionately grieved feels anger and disappointment, as if their right to be completely dead has been stolen from them. So it would be improper for a villager to display the kind of restraint and solemnity seen at Western funerals.'

There must be many angry souls lost and wandering around. It is this sense of disconnection between us and our ancestors that has contributed to some of the problems we have in society. Of course, this is a huge generalisation about the West, but this does seem to be an issue that's alive within our communities. This disengagement from death, the dead and grieving when in fact quite the opposite is true. We are still connected and actually we need each other. The mistakes and pain of our ancestors are still alive within us and we have an opportunity to resolve and release this.

Ways to connect and help the grieving process

There are different things you can do to honour your grieving process. Altar work can be a good way to do this.

When a loved one passes I light a candle and put it on my altar and I burn incense for them every day and play music that they liked. I speak to them, tell them I love them, and that they are dead. I tell them how happy I was to have had the privilege to know them. I tell them to go towards the light. Take time to cry if it comes and just be there with the process.

In the Shamanic Korean Bardo tradition, they say the soul wanders for 49 days until rebirth and that prayers and ceremonies done by the living help to support them with their transition. If someone passes away that was close to me, I keep an electric candle lit for them for 49 days.

If you shared family and friends with the deceased then think about meeting up at regular intervals that suit you. You can share memories, cry, share your grief or even just be quiet together. If others are also spiritual, you could create rituals together and do altar work.

Building an altar for your ancestors and deceased loved ones.

Mexico is famous for its extravagant Day of the Dead celebrations; incredible altars are built and the festive events are enjoyed. The main time for the rituals is on the 1st and 2nd of November. The veil between the living and dying is said to open on the 1st with the children coming first and it closes again in the night of the 2nd. Check with your local traditions and ancestry too as dates may vary and go with what suits you. For example, if I wanted to stick with my Chinese ancestry, I would do it in April.

Create an altar as if creating a party for your ancestors. Choose a nice tablecloth, food, dessert or sweets, drink, flowers, balloons, decorations for the altar and room, and anything you know that people would like. Sprinkle flower petals from the altar up to the door that is the entrance to your place. The dead can see these petals and follow them. Put pictures of whoever you want to come. If you don't have a picture use a skull to represent them with their name on it. It doesn't matter what it's made of and place a candle in

Below is an example of altar using marigold flowers, sugar skulls and offerings. Colour is also used to express the celebration of your ancestor's life.

front of each person's skull or picture as they come searching for the light. Play some music that you like or knew that they liked.

A few words about etiquette! Make sure you turn up. Don't suddenly leave. Make sure you are paying them proper attention. Make sure there is something for everyone's tastes on the altar. Just as if you were hosting a party for the living.

You can set up and keep a permanent altar for your ancestors.

EXERCISE TO CONNECT WITH AN ANCESTOR

This exercise is also inspired by Mexican practices with the dead and it is to connect with a known or unknown ancestor.

◎ Choose the person you wish to connect with. You may simply wish to connect to honour them or because there were problems and they may need some assistance.

◎ Take a photo of them. If that's not available then take a skull-shaped object. It can be made of plastic, crystal or anything you have available. The skull is symbolic of human consciousness.

◎ Create an altar for them. Put out offerings of flowers, food and drink (if you knew them, pick their favourites).

◎ Light a candle and place it in front of the photo/skull so their consciousness knows where to go.

◎ Say their name out loud or, if you don't know their name, just say Great Grandfather, Great Aunt, inviting their consciousness into the photo or skull. For example, 'Sarah, please come into this skull.'

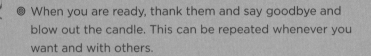

- Look into the skull/photo and say their name. Tell them that they are dead and that they are loved. Say whatever you would like to say to them. If you didn't know them, introduce yourself. Tell them who you are and that you're honoured to make a connection with them. If this was a difficult relationship, say what you feel you need to say to them. This can bring surprising shifts.

- When you are ready, thank them and say goodbye and blow out the candle. This can be repeated whenever you want and with others.

Facing our mortality

A common sign of shamanic election is the near death experience, as discussed on page 14. This experience brings into sharp focus our mortality and gives us a stronger connection to the spirit world. I'm sure there will be many of you reading this who have had near death experiences or have been in a situation where you were 'lucky to get out alive'. Whether or not you have, it can be a valuable exercise to meditate upon death and our mortality. Become aware of the ever-present possibility that we largely do not get to choose the timing of our death. It is so easy for us to forget this and have a kind of unspoken assumption that we are immortal, but reinforcing this awareness can make us appreciate life much more fully and passionately. It enables us to not waste time or take life and each other for granted. The journey opposite is inspired by the Egyptian Book of the Dead.

DEATH AND REBIRTH JOURNEY

For this I recommend you lie down on the floor. Make sure you won't be disturbed. You may want to play a longer track of shamanic drumming or music (nothing too happy or distracting). Burn incense to create a stronger altered state. The more you can immerse yourself in this exercise and suspend your disbelief, the more profound it will be for you. If it's easier you may want to record it or get someone to read it out with pauses so you can just listen to it. Give yourself time afterwards to integrate. Don't rush off to go somewhere!

◎ Lie down on the floor to begin.

◎ You are about to die.

◎ You are dying to be reborn.

◎ Focus your attention on your heart and your breath.

◎ Feel your heart beating in the centre of your chest. Slow down your breath and, with your will and mind, slow your heartbeat down.

◎ Spend some time doing this. This is not to be rushed.

- ◎ Eventually your heartbeat and breath will become more imperceptible.

- ◎ Feel a type of paralysis set into your body. You are dying.

- ◎ You are dying to everything you were, everything you did, everything you had.

- ◎ Your life as you knew it is over.

- ◎ Death comes to all of us. None of us know when or how it will happen.

◎ Your consciousness – your life force – is leaving your body. Feel it leaving your body. You are no longer your body, but you can see your body.

◎ Six beings enter and they have surgical tools. They remove all of your organs, except your heart.

◎ Another being, a guide for you, enters the room ready to escort your soul into the afterlife.

◎ They take you into a room of beaming golden light with a fountain in it containing glistening crystalline white water. They ask you questions, but they ask them directly to your heart. You hear your heart answer each question honestly.

◎ 'How did you treat others in your thoughts, words and actions?'

◎ 'Did you enjoy your life?'

◎ 'Did you fulfil your life purpose?'

◎ 'If you could go back, what would you do differently?'

◎ Take a moment to be aware of how you feel. Do you feel any sense of regret or maybe surprise or contentment? Feel the heaviness or lightness in your heart. Try not to judge, just observe.

◎ The being reaches into your chest and takes out your heart. They hold it in the fountain.

◎ Feel any heaviness, anger or regret washing away in these sacred waters and fill up with beautiful, pure light as they place your heart back into your chest.

◎ They tell you that you are not ready to cross over yet and you are going back, but that you must not forget what was discussed here.

◎ You have died to your old self and will not go back as the same person.

◎ The being escorts you back to the room where your body is and you feel yourself back in your body.

◎ The six beings are there with your organs. They have been purified and cleansed like your heart and they put them back inside your body.

◎ Thank the beings for this valuable experience and lesson.

◎ Begin to become more aware of your breath and feel the sense of paralysis lifting from your physical body.

◎ Feel your organs new and purified inside your body.

◎ You have been reborn new.

◎ When you are ready, open your eyes. See the world anew for the first time. Hear with fresh ears.

◎ Take your time to move around and enjoy your new body and life.

◎ You may want to note down your experience. Really take time to feel and integrate this experience.

I challenge you to take at least one action based on this experience. It may be a conversation, a decision or fulfilling a dream. Take some form of action within a week of doing this exercise.

Enjoy your new life!

CHAPTER 10

The future of shamanism

Although shamanism is as old as humanity, there is an ever-growing interest and appetite for it as people want to reconnect with our spiritual roots. Its form is morphing and changing with the times. Unbroken traditions that still exist must be preserved with the utmost care because much precious knowledge that is highly sophisticated can be lost. We do not want to lose touch with the roots of where this has all come from. However, I would encourage embracing changes as this is the nature of life.

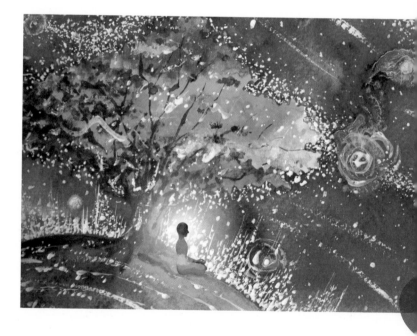

There are growing numbers of digital devices and wearables that claim to alter mind states and brain wave frequency. Some people even claim to have out-of-body experiences with them. Although the effectiveness seems to vary with different people, this is clearly an area that is making advances. This could have an effect on the experience of journeying and dreaming for some.

The internet has had a radical influence on the availability of knowledge. It seems vast pools of knowledge that would have been virtually inaccessible to most people are ready and waiting at the click of a button. Conference calls and webinars have made it possible to hold shamanic ceremony internationally. Although this is also possible without computers simply by agreed distance work with your healer or group. This gives scope for wider possibilities. Shamanic groups hold prayers internationally for world disasters. We are now spreading the work into a wider web creating a healing matrix globally. This is also why cultural boundaries seem to be blurring more and more. Purists don't always agree with this increasingly syncretic approach. Care does need to be taken to see that practices are not compatible with each other, causing energetic sickness, particularly when working with various methods of cultivating and circulating energy. But it seems that some kind of melding is becoming inevitable with the way the world is now for many of us. This is also in alignment with the rainbow warriors prophesy of the Hopis:

'There will come a day when people of all races, colours and creeds will put aside their differences. They will come together in love, joining hands in unification, to heal the Earth and all Her children. They will move all over the Earth like a great Whirling Rainbow, bringing peace, understanding and healing wherever they go. Many creatures thought to be extinct or mythical will resurface at this time; the great trees that perished will return almost overnight. All living things will flourish, drawing sustenance from the Earth, our Mother.'

Another prophesy from the Incans speaks of the divide between the modern, rationalist, materialistic cultures represented by the Eagle, and the older, more heart-based, nature-based ways of living, represented by the Condor coming together.

'When the Eagle of the North flies with the Condor of the South, the spirit of the land she will re-awaken.'

We are also, according to the Aztec/Toltec calendar tradition, on the crest of entering a new stage of the Sixth Sun in 2021 which lasts for 6,625 years. The Sun that we are presently leaving, the fifth Sun, was a time of 'outward' focus. The divine was perceived to be outside us in religious buildings and we looked outwardly towards spiritual authorities such as priests and gurus. Whereas the sixth Sun is about the 'inner' experience so self-exploration, reflection and dream work will be key during this time. Healing and medicine will be sought within ourselves. I think that we can already see this happening. This can also explain why so much knowledge has become so accessible because it is time for our self-empowerment and self-responsibility. Sergio Magaña teaches about the meaning of the Sixth Sun in his book *2012-2021: The Dawn of the Sixth Sun*:

'...if the Fifth Sun, for instance, was a Sun of the Tonal whose luminosity drove humankind to look externally for everything that is visible in the illusion of the day, namely in conquests and relationships, thus projecting their existence mainly outside themselves, a Sun ruled by darkness entails that the night and its forces, the dream realm (the "*unknown*"), will be governing forces and therefore the gaze of humans will be turned inwards.'

The late author and shamanic practitioner Ross Heaven heals a patient using elements of darkness and light.

JOURNEY TO A FUTURE SELF

Let's finish our time together with a journey to a future version of yourself with a message or insight that will benefit you now. This will be a Middle World journey.

State your intention three times:

> **I am going to the Middle World
> to meet a future version of myself** (if
> you have an area of inquiry, such as
> your relationships or your career or
> where to live, name it here)
> **for guidance.**

◎ See yourself at the World Tree, then go behind the tree. As I said earlier, I go via a wall that I run through but others might see a forest that they can walk through – choose the imagery that works best for you. The transition is fast as it's on our level.

◎ See yourself in a clearing. Your Middle World future self is there.

◎ If you have something specific you would like to know, ask it. Otherwise see what you have to tell yourself.

◎ When the drum call-back comes, prepare to come back.

◎ If you give yourself something, then physically put your arms out above your heart and bring the gift into your heart.

◎ Give thanks to your future self and for the journey.

◎ Come back into your body, making sure you feel fully grounded and 'in your body'.

◎ If you have a rattle and were given something, it's good to shake the rattle around your heart and your whole body three times to integrate the new energy.

◎ Have some quiet time to integrate the experience. Write down the journey in your journal.

Happy explorations and may your world be full of magic!

Further reading

BOOKS

Andrews, Ted *Animal Speak* (Llewellyn Publications, 1993)

Castaneda Carlos *The Teachings of Don Juan: A Yaqui Way of Knowledge* (Penguin, 1974)

Chia, Mantak & North, Kris Deva *Taoist Shaman* (Destiny books, 2009)

Denney, Michael William *Shamanism for "White"people* (Self-published, 2012)

Eliade, Mircea *Shamanism: Archaic Techniques of Ecstasy* (Princeton University Press, 1964)

Greenfield, Trevor *What is Shamanism?* (Moon books, 2018)

Heaven, Ross *Medicine for the Soul* (Moon books, 2012)

Heaven, Ross *Plant Spirit Shamanism* (Destiny Books, 2006)

Magaña, Sergio (Ocelocoyotl) *2012-2021 The Dawn of the Sixth Sun* (Blossoming books, 2012)

Magaña, Sergio (Ocelocoytl) *Caves of Power* (Hay House, 2016)

Roth, Gabrielle *Maps to Ecstasy* (Crucible, 1990)

Some, Malidoma Patrice *Of Water and the Spirit* (Penguin group, 1994)

Vitebsky, Piers *The Shaman* (Duncan Baird Publishers, 1995)

ONLINE RESOURCES

britishacademyofsoundtherapy.com

shamanism.org

5rhythms.com